40-Minute
BIBLE STUDIES

6-Week
Study Program

HOW DO YOU

——

KNOW

——

GOD'S YOUR

——

FATHER?

——

PRECEPT
MINISTRIES
INTERNATIONAL

Kay Arthur
David & BJ Lawson

How Do You Know God's Your Father?
Published by WaterBrook Press
2375 Telstar Drive, Suite 160
Colorado Springs, Colorado 80920
A division of Random House, Inc.

All Scripture quotations, unless otherwise indicated, are taken from the *New American Standard Bible®* (NASB). © Copyright The Lockman Foundation 1960, 1962, 1963, 1968, 1971, 1972, 1973, 1975, 1977, 1995. Used by permission. (www.Lockman.org)

Italics in Scripture quotations reflect the author's added emphasis.

ISBN 1-57856-478-6

Printed in the United States of America
2001—First Edition

10 9 8 7 6 5 4 3 2 1

HOW TO USE THIS STUDY

This small-group study is for people who are interested in learning more about what the Bible says, but who have only limited time to meet together. It's ideal, for example, for a lunch group at work, an early morning men's group, a young mother's group meeting in a home, or a smaller Sunday-school class. (It's also ideal for small groups that typically have longer meeting times—such as evening groups or Saturday morning groups—but want to devote only a portion of their time together to actual study, while reserving the rest for prayer, fellowship, or other activities.)

This book is designed so that all the group's participants will complete each lesson's study activities *at the same time, while you're together.*

However, you'll need a facilitator to lead the group—someone to keep the discussion moving. (This person's function is *not* that of a lecturer or teacher. However, when this book is used in a Sunday-school class or similar setting, the teacher should feel free to lead more directly and to bring in other insights in addition to those provided in each week's lesson.)

If *you* are your group's facilitator, the leader, here are some helpful points for making your job easier:

- Go through the lesson and mark the text before you lead the group. This will give you increased familiarity with the material and will enable you to facilitate the group with greater ease. It may be easier for you to lead the group through the instructions for marking if you as a leader choose a specific color for each symbol you mark.

- As you lead the group, start at the beginning of the text and simply read it aloud in the order it appears in the lesson, including the "insight boxes," which may appear either before or after the instructions or in the midst of your observations or discussion. Work through the lesson together, observing and discussing what you learn. As you read the Scripture verses, have the group say aloud the word they are marking in the text.

- The discussion questions are there simply to help you cover the material. As the class moves into the discussion, many times you will find that they will cover the questions on their own. Remember the discussion questions are there to guide the group through the topic, not to squelch discussion.

- Remember how important it is for people to verbalize their answers and discoveries. This greatly strengthens their personal understanding of each week's lesson. Try to ensure that everyone has plenty of opportunity to contribute to each week's discussions.

- Keep the discussion moving. This may mean spending more time on some parts of the study than on others. If necessary, you should feel free to spread out a lesson over more than one session. However, remember that you don't want to slow the pace too much. It's much better to leave everyone "wanting more" than to have people dropping out because of declining interest.

- If the validity or accuracy of some of the answers seems questionable, you can gently and cheerfully remind the group to stay focused on the truth of the Scriptures. Your object is to learn what the Bible says, not to engage in human philosophy. Really *read* the Scriptures, asking God to show everyone His answers.

HOW DO YOU KNOW GOD'S YOUR FATHER?

During Jesus' ministry He turned to some religious leaders and said, "You are of your father the devil" (John 8:44). What an affront that must have been to men who thought they had God as their father.

What does a genuine Christian look like? Have you ever wondered? And what about you? Are you a Christian? Do you know you are going to heaven? Or can a person know for sure?

We have often counseled people who are struggling with doubts about their relationship with God. It is a miserable way to live—always wondering, always hoping, but never certain. They have no joy, no peace, no confidence—only anguish.

With eternity hanging in the balance, you need to know where you stand with God. In other words, who's your father—God or the devil?

For the next six weeks we will study 1 John together and seek answers to this question. Sometimes the truth will excite you, sometimes you will praise God for revealing Himself to you, and sometimes the truth will make you uncomfortable. Very uncomfortable. The truth does that. But please don't quit; the truth will also set you free.

One of Jesus' disciples, John, wrote five of the books in the Bible. One of them, a letter known as 1 John, was written to answer our question: "How do you know God's your Father?" We'll begin our study by letting John tell us exactly why he wrote this letter.

OBSERVE

Leader: *Read aloud 1 John 1:1-4; 2:1-2,26; and 5:13, reprinted for you in the sidebars on pages 3-5.*

• *Underline the words **write, writing,** or **written** with a squiggly line like this:*

~~~~~~~

Have the group say aloud the words they are marking. This way no one will miss marking the word. Do this throughout the study.

DISCUSS

• Look at each place you have marked the word *write*. According to these verses, why is John writing this letter? What are the reasons he gives?

1 John 1:1-4

1 What was from the beginning, what we have heard, what we have seen with our eyes, what we have looked at and touched with our hands, concerning the Word of Life—

2 and the life was manifested, and we have seen and testify and proclaim to you the eternal life, which was with the Father and was manifested to us—

³ what we have seen and heard we proclaim to you also, so that you too may have fellowship with us; and indeed our fellowship is with the Father, and with His Son Jesus Christ.

⁴ These things we write, so that our joy may be made complete.

1 JOHN 2:1-2

¹ My little children, I am writing these things to you so that you may not sin. And if anyone sins, we have an Advocate with the Father, Jesus Christ the righteous;

² and He Himself is the propitiation for our sins; and not for ours only, but also for those of the whole world.

• What's the last reason John gives in 1 John 5:13?

• Why do you think it was important that his readers know that they have eternal life?

• What does 1 John 5:13 tell you about eternal life? So many people say you won't know if you'll get into heaven until you stand before God and He weighs the good against the bad. According to 1 John 5:13, is that true?

1 John 2:26

These things I have written to you concerning those who are trying to deceive you.

1 John 5:13

These things I have written to you who believe in the name of the Son of God, so that you may know that you have eternal life.

1 JOHN 1:1-3

1 What was from the beginning, what we have heard, what we have seen with our eyes, what we have looked at and touched with our hands, concerning the Word of Life—

2 and the life was manifested, and we have seen and testify and proclaim to you the eternal life, which was with the Father and was manifested to us—

3 what we have seen and heard we proclaim to you also, so that you too may have fellowship with us; and indeed our fellowship is with the Father, and with His Son Jesus Christ.

OBSERVE

Leader: Read aloud 1 John 1:1-3 again. This time instruct the group to mark...
- *every reference to the **author** by putting a box around every **we** and **our:***
- ***the Word of Life** (which is a reference to Jesus Christ) and any other synonyms with a cross:* ✝

DISCUSS

- What do you learn about John from marking references to *we* and *our*?

- What do you learn from marking the references to *Jesus Christ*, the Word of Life?

- Why do you think John is telling this to the recipients of this letter? What would this information do for them? Does it mean anything to you?

OBSERVE

Leader: Read 1 John 1:5-10. Have the group say aloud and mark:

- *every reference to **God** (including **Him**, **He**, and **His**) with a triangle, like this:*

  △

- *every reference to **Jesus Christ** with a cross:* ✝

Now read through the text again and mark:

- *every occurrence of **darkness** and **light**. Circle both words, then put a slash through darkness, like this:* ⬭
- *the word **sin(s)** by drawing a large **S** over it.*

Read through 1 John 1:5-10 once more. This time have the group mark:

- *every **we** and **us** with a box.*
- ***fellowship**, like this:*

INSIGHT

The Greek word for *fellowship* is *koinonia,* which means "to share in common." Someone has said, "It's two fellows in the same ship!"

1 JOHN 1:5-10

⁵ This is the message we have heard from Him and announce to you, that God is Light, and in Him there is no darkness at all.

⁶ If we say that we have fellowship with Him and yet walk in the darkness, we lie and do not practice the truth;

⁷ but if we walk in the Light as He Himself is in the Light, we have fellowship with one another, and the blood of Jesus His Son cleanses us from all sin.

⁸ If we say that we have no sin, we are deceiving ourselves and the truth is not in us.

⁹ If we confess our sins, He is faithful and righteous to forgive us our sins and to cleanse us from all unrighteousness.

¹⁰ If we say that we have not sinned, we make Him a liar and His word is not in us.

DISCUSS

• What did you learn from marking *God*?

• What do you learn from marking *fellowship*?

• What two things are true, according to verse 7, if we walk in the light?

• If you have sin, how are you to deal with it? (Look at the places you marked *sin* with an *S.*)

• What happens if I confess my sin? What two things does God do if I confess my sins?

OBSERVE

Leader: *Read aloud the Insight Box on sin.*

INSIGHT

There are a number of verses in the Bible that define sin for us.

Sin is...

- breaking God's law.
- refusing to believe in Jesus.
- knowing to do good and not doing it.
- lawlessness.
- not operating on the basis of faith.
- going our own way.
- missing the mark, falling short of God's standard.

DISCUSS

- Do you know anyone who claims to be a Christian but walks in darkness as a habit of his or her life? What does 1 John 1:5-10 tell you about this person?

MATTHEW 5:14-16

[Jesus is speaking]

14 "You are the light of the world. A city set on a hill cannot be hidden;

15 "nor does anyone light a lamp and put it under a basket, but on the lampstand, and it gives light to all who are in the house.

16 "Let your light shine before men in such a way that they may see your good works, and glorify your Father who is in heaven."

OBSERVE

God is light and in Him there is no darkness at all. Those who claim God as their father should walk in the light as He is in the light. Jesus spoke about the light in a sermon He preached, which we refer to as the Sermon on the Mount. We don't have time to read the entire sermon; however, we do want to look at a small part of it to see what we can learn about light.

Leader: Read aloud Matthew 5:14-16. Have the group say aloud the words they are marking.
- *Mark every reference to **light** with a circle just as you have been doing.*
- *Underline every **you** and **your**.*

DISCUSS

- What did you learn by marking the word *light*?

- If God is my Father, what will bring Him glory?

• How do we let our light shine before others?

• From all you have learned today, how important is the way we live?

• Does our lifestyle show or demonstrate our relationship with God or our lack of relationship with God?

• How about those who sit in church and profess to know God? How do they measure up to what you've learned about a genuine relationship with God?

• How do you measure up?

WRAP IT UP

John was an eyewitness of the life, death, and resurrection of Jesus Christ. He was a disciple, a student of Jesus. He was even one of the select group of twelve, an apostle. He had a commission from Jesus Christ to speak and to write with His authority. We are studying the words of a man who knew Jesus intimately, personally. He walked with Him, ate with Him, and listened to Him as He taught. What John has written is inspired by God and without any error at all. Therefore we need to hear and heed what the Holy Spirit says.

God is light and in Him there is no darkness at all. Those who claim to have fellowship with Him must walk in the light. The question is, are you walking in the light? To walk in the light is to live your life in such a way that, no matter who is watching, you never have reason to be ashamed of what you are doing. Are you letting your light shine before men in such a way that they see your good works and glorify God?

The apostle John, in writing this letter, wants us to know whether or not we have eternal life. Everything we study in this letter relates to this purpose. You need to know. You must know. Eternity hangs in the balance. Do you have eternal life? Are you walking in the light?

Next week we will continue in our study of 1 John. We will learn more about the characteristics of a child of God and, by comparison, the characteristics of a child of the devil.

Last week we learned about walking in the light. This week we'll continue our study by going into 1 John 2, where we'll learn more about light and darkness and about knowing God and abiding in Him.

OBSERVE

Leader: Read 1 John 2:1-6 aloud. Have the group do the following:

- *Mark **sin(s)** with a big **S**, including pronouns.*
- *Mark every reference to **Jesus Christ**, including the pronouns, with a cross:* ✝

Now read it one more time and do the following:

- *Mark every occurrence of **abides**. Since the word "abide" means "to dwell in, to be at home in," use this symbol:* ⌂
- *Mark **know** with a big **K.***

DISCUSS

- According to verse 1, why is John writing?

- What do you learn from marking references to Jesus Christ?

1 JOHN 2:1-6

1 My little children, I am writing these things to you so that you may not sin. And if anyone sins, we have an Advocate with the Father, Jesus Christ the righteous;

2 and He Himself is the propitiation for our sins; and not for ours only, but also for those of the whole world.

3 By this we know that we have come to know Him, if we keep His commandments.

4 The one who says, "I have come to know Him," and does not keep His commandments, is a liar, and the truth is not in him;

5 but whoever keeps His word, in him the love of God has truly been perfected. By this we know that we are in Him:

6 the one who says he abides in Him ought himself to walk in the same manner as He walked.

INSIGHT

An "advocate" is a supporter, someone who is on our side. A lawyer is sometimes referred to as an advocate.

In the Old Testament the place in the tabernacle where God met man was called the "mercy seat," or the "propitiation." To say Jesus is our "propitiation" is to say that *He* is where we meet God and where our sins are forgiven.

• What do you learn from marking *know*? What do you know and how?

OBSERVE

Leader: *Read 1 John 2:4-6 again.*

    • *Underline* **the one who says** *like this:*

DISCUSS

• What do you learn from marking *the one who says*?

OBSERVE

So far we have seen that walking in the light and keeping His commandments are characteristics of a child of God. John also said that the one who abides in Christ Jesus ought to walk as Christ walked. But how did Christ walk? Can we really walk like He did?

Let's look at this idea and see what Scripture says.

Leader: Read John 5:19 and 8:28 aloud.
 • *Mark each reference to **Jesus** with a cross.*
 • *Double underline every reference to **do, doing,** and **does.***

DISCUSS

• What do you learn from marking *Jesus*?

• If you walk as Jesus walked, what would you seek to do?

JOHN 5:19

Therefore Jesus answered and was saying to them, "Truly, truly, I say to you, the Son can do nothing of Himself, unless it is something He sees the Father doing; for whatever the Father does, these things the Son also does in like manner."

JOHN 8:28

So Jesus said, "When you lift up the Son of Man, then you will know that I am *He,* and I do nothing on My own initiative, but I speak these things as the Father taught Me."

1 JOHN 2:9-11

⁹ The one who says he is in the Light and yet hates his brother is in the darkness until now.

¹⁰ The one who loves his brother abides in the Light and there is no cause for stumbling in him.

¹¹ But the one who hates his brother is in the darkness and walks in the darkness, and does not know where he is going because the darkness has blinded his eyes.

OBSERVE

Leader: *Read 1 John 2:9-11 aloud. Have the group say the words aloud as they mark:*
- ***light*** ⬭ *and* ***darkness*** ⬭ *as you did previously.*
- *references to* ***love*** ♡ *and* ***hate*** ♡
- ***abides*** *with a house as before:* ⌂

Leader: *Read aloud the Insight Box.*

INSIGHT

In Greek, the language of the New Testament, verbs in the present tense generally mean a continuous, ongoing, or habitual action. The perfect tense for Greek verbs generally means an action was completed in the past, while the results of that action are continuing to the present.

In 1 John 2:9, the Greek word for *hates* is in the present tense. Therefore, this passage isn't referring to a single event of hatred but to an ongoing pattern.

The Greek verb for *loves* in 1 John 2:10 is also in the present tense, as is *abides*.

DISCUSS

- What are the characteristics of someone who walks in darkness?

- What are the characteristics of someone who walks in the light?

- You learned in 1 John 1:5-6 that God is light. Where do those who know God walk?

- What is the relationship between love and light?

- What is the relationship between hate and darkness?

- What does a Christian look like, according to this passage? What does a non-Christian look like, according to this passage?

- Are you walking in love for your brother?

LUKE 6:31-35

31 "Treat others in the same way you want them to treat you.

32 "If you love those who love you, what credit is that to you? For even sinners love those who love them.

33 "If you do good to those who do good to you, what credit is that to you? For even sinners do the same.

34 "If you lend to those from whom you expect to receive, what credit is that to you? Even sinners lend to sinners in order to receive back the same amount.

OBSERVE

Who is your "brother"? In this letter John probably has in mind fellow Christians as "brothers in the Lord." A characteristic of those who have eternal life is that they act in love toward fellow believers. So does this mean we can hate those outside the community of faith? To answer this question let's look at the words of Jesus in the following passage.

Leader: As you read Luke 6:31-35, have the group say aloud and mark...

- *love with a heart just as you have been doing.*
- *every occurrence of even sinners with an S and then underline it.*
- *every reference to God with a triangle:*
  $\triangle$

DISCUSS

- What did you learn from marking *love*?

- How are we to treat others?

• What do you learn about God from these verses?

35 "But love your enemies, and do good, and lend, expecting nothing in return; and your reward will be great, and you will be sons of the Most High; for He Himself is kind to ungrateful and evil men."

• According to this passage, what is a follower of Jesus Christ to do? To whom? Why?

• If there's time, summarize what you've learned this week about God's children.

• Now what have you learned personally this week?

WRAP IT UP

To abide in Christ means to be at home with Him—to dwell in Him, to have Him living in you.

One characteristic of abiding in Christ is walking in love. The biblical idea of love is more than just an emotion; it involves meeting needs. To love our brother (or another) is to meet his needs. What does your brother need? Acceptance? A friend? Understanding? Someone to tell him the truth—gently, in love?

Are you loving the people God has placed in your life? Are you meeting their needs? Or are you just trying to look out for your own needs?

What would Jesus do? He would do what He saw His Father do. God so loved the whole world that He gave His only Son. Selfless giving and kindness are characteristics of God the Father. How different this is from Satan, who is a murderer (John 8:44)!

You have covered a lot of material this week. May the Lord bless you and keep you, and may you walk in love.

Last week we saw that someone who "hates his brother" is walking in darkness, while someone who "loves his brother" is walking in the light. God is very serious about our relationship with others. Perhaps in years past you saw one of the billboards that read, "That part about loving your neighbor, I meant that." It was signed, "God." This week we'll learn even more about loving, knowing, and abiding.

OBSERVE

Leader: *Read 1 John 2:15-17 aloud.*
> • *Mark the word* **love** *with a heart as you have before, and have the group say it aloud as you come to it.*

DISCUSS

• What do you learn from marking *love* in this passage?

• According to these verses, what do you think it means to love the world?

1 JOHN 2:15-17

15 Do not love the world nor the things in the world. If anyone loves the world, the love of the Father is not in him.

16 For all that is in the world, the lust of the flesh and the lust of the eyes and the boastful pride of life, is not from the Father, but is from the world.

17 The world is passing away, and also its lusts; but the one who does the will of God lives forever.

GENESIS 3:1-6

1 Now the serpent was more crafty than any beast of the field which the LORD God had made. And he said to the woman, "Indeed, has God said, 'You shall not eat from any tree of the garden'?"

2 The woman said to the serpent, "From the fruit of the trees of the garden we may eat;

3 but from the fruit of the tree which is in the middle of the garden, God has said, 'You shall not eat from it or touch it, or you will die.'"

• What do you think is meant by "the lust of the flesh and the lust of the eyes and the boastful pride of life" (verse 16)? Are these three things characteristic of the lives of many who profess Christ? What about your life?

• Do you battle with a love for the world? How?

• According to this passage, who will live forever?

OBSERVE

There is an Old Testament passage that illustrates 1 John 2:16 perfectly. As you read Genesis 3:1-6, keep in mind the things John tells us that are in the world and are not from the Father: "the lust of the flesh, the lust of the eyes, and the boastful pride of life."

Leader: *Read Genesis 3:1-6 aloud.*

    • *Mark every reference to the **serpent** with a pitchfork:*

• *Mark every reference to the **woman** like this:* ♀

DISCUSS

• What did Eve say she and Adam were forbidden to do?

• What did the serpent say to entice the woman to eat the fruit of the tree?

• What did the serpent appeal to in Eve?

• Look carefully at verse 6. Is there anything there that would correspond to
   "the lust of the flesh"?
   "the lust of the eyes"?
   "the boastful pride of life"?
   What is it?

Eve listened to the serpent—she took of the forbidden fruit and gave it to Adam. They both ate and on that day they both became sinners. The wages of their sin was death.

4 The serpent said to the woman, "You surely will not die!

5 "For God knows that in the day you eat from it your eyes will be opened, and you will be like God, knowing good and evil."

6 When the woman saw that the tree was good for food, and that it was a delight to the eyes, and that the tree was desirable to make one wise, she took from its fruit and ate; and she gave also to her husband with her, and he ate.

REVELATION 12:9

And the great dragon was thrown down, the serpent of old who is called the devil and Satan, who deceives the whole world; he was thrown down to the earth, and his angels were thrown down with him.

JOHN 8:44

You are of your father the devil, and you want to do the desires of your father. He was a murderer from the beginning, and does not stand in the truth because there is no truth in him. Whenever he speaks a lie, he speaks from his own nature, for he is a liar and the father of lies.

• How does our society, our world encourage "the lust of the flesh"?

"the lust of the eyes"?

"the boastful pride of life"?

OBSERVE

Who was the serpent and what is he like? His identity and character are revealed in the following scriptures.

Leader: Have the group read Revelation 12:9 and John 8:44.

> • *Mark every reference to the **devil** with a pitchfork, like this:* ⚰

DISCUSS

• What did you learn about the devil, the serpent of old, from these scriptures?

OBSERVE

Leader: Read 1 John 2:18-29.

- *Mark every reference to **knowing** with a big* **K**.
- *Mark every reference to **abiding** as you have done before:* ⌂ *In verse 19, the word **remained** is a synonym for the word "abide," so be sure to mark it just as you would "abide."*
- *Mark **antichrist** like this:* ✗

DISCUSS

- What do you learn from marking the references to *abiding* and *remaining*?

- What are the characteristics of a believer, according to verses 23 and 29?

- What do you learn from marking references to the antichrist?

1 JOHN 2:18-29

18 Children, it is the last hour; and just as you heard that antichrist is coming, even now many antichrists have appeared; from this we know that it is the last hour.

19 They went out from us, but they were not really of us; for if they had been of us, they would have remained with us; but they went out, so that it would be shown that they all are not of us.

20 But you have an anointing from the Holy One, and you all know.

21 I have not written to you because you do not know the truth, but because you do know it, and because no lie is of the truth.

22 Who is the liar but the one who denies that Jesus is the Christ? This is the antichrist, the one who denies the Father and the Son.

23 Whoever denies the Son does not have the Father; the one who confesses the Son has the Father also.

24 As for you, let that abide in you which you heard from the beginning. If what you heard from the beginning abides in you, you also will abide in the Son and in the Father.

25 This is the promise which He Himself made to us: eternal life.

26 These things I have written to you concerning those who are trying to deceive you.

• According to verse 19, when someone claims to be a Christian then walks away from the faith, was he ever a Christian to begin with? Why does a person walk away, leave Christianity?

• Who are those who remain?

• John gives one of his reasons for writing this letter in verse 26. Why does he write?

• How are "the antichrists" trying to deceive the recipients of this letter?

• In verse 28, what is the command John gives? Why?

• According to verse 29, if you are born of God, God is your Father. What will you practice?

INSIGHT

Righteousness is conformity to God's standard, commandments, and precepts—His will. It is to do what is right. It is saying to God, "I will honor you as God. I will live the way You want me to live."

---

27 As for you, the anointing which you received from Him abides in you, and you have no need for anyone to teach you; but as His anointing teaches you about all things, and is true and is not a lie, and just as it has taught you, you abide in Him.

28 Now, little children, abide in Him, so that when He appears, we may have confidence and not shrink away from Him in shame at His coming.

29 If you know that He is righteous, you know that everyone also who practices righteousness is born of Him.

WRAP IT UP

Every true child of God has "an anointing from the Holy One," and this is what enables us to know truth. This anointing abides on us—and thus God is able to teach us Himself and to affirm to us that we are His children. His Spirit bears witness with our spirit that we are children of God.

If you have this anointing, Beloved, His Spirit is within and you will never walk away from God, as we have seen in 1 John 2:20,27. You may stray at times, but if you are His child, you will always come back. So hold fast your confession of faith. Abide in Him, and you will not shrink back at Jesus' return.

And what will be the characteristics of your life? That we will see next week as we look at how great a love the Father has bestowed upon us—and how His love within confirms He is our Father.

We learned about abiding last week. Are you abiding in the truth? Are you abiding in Christ? This week we'll look at 1 John 3. As you read and study, we're praying that the Holy Spirit will make the passages come alive to you. God promised the Holy Spirit would lead us into truth. Why don't you claim that promise in prayer before you start this lesson?

OBSERVE

Leader: Read 1 John 3:1-12. As before, have the group say aloud and mark...

- *the word **sin(s)** with a large* **S.**
- *the word **love** with a heart.*

Now read through 1 John 3:1-12 again and have the group mark...

- *every occurrence of the phrase **children of God** like this:* <u>children of God</u>
- *every occurrence of the phrase **children of the devil** like this:* <u>children of the devil</u>
- *the word **know** with a large* **K.**

1 JOHN 3:1-12

1 See how great a love the Father has bestowed on us, that we would be called children of God; and such we are. For this reason the world does not know us, because it did not know Him.

2 Beloved, now we are children of God, and it has not appeared as yet what we will be. We know that when He appears, we will be like Him, because we will see Him just as He is.

3 And everyone who has this hope fixed on Him purifies himself, just as He is pure.

4 Everyone who practices sin also practices lawlessness; and sin is lawlessness.

5 You know that He appeared in order to take away sins; and in Him there is no sin.

6 No one who abides in Him sins; no one who sins has seen Him or knows Him.

7 Little children, make sure no one deceives you; the one who practices righteousness is righteous, just as He is righteous;

INSIGHT

The verb tenses are very important in 1 John 3 because they help clarify what God is saying about the children of God and the children of the devil. The word *practices* in this passage indicates a present tense verb, implying continuous or habitual action. This means, as you know, a pattern of behavior or a lifestyle.

DISCUSS

• If my hope for eternal life is fixed on Christ, what am I going to do, according to verse 3?

• How would a person living in this world, which is in such opposition to God, purify him- or herself?

• According to verse 4, what's true of someone who "practices" (present tense) sin?

- Why did Christ appear, according to verse 5? Is there any sin in Him?

- In verse 6, both occurrences of the word *sins* are in the present tense. What does this tell you?

- Also in verse 6, the words *seen* and *knows* are perfect tense, which indicates a past completed action with a present or continuous result. What does this tell you?

- In verse 7, the one who "practices" (present tense) righteousness is what?

- Are you practicing righteousness? Explain what righteousness is.

- What do you learn about one who "practices" (present tense) sin, according to verse 8?

8 the one who practices sin is of the devil; for the devil has sinned from the beginning. The Son of God appeared for this purpose, to destroy the works of the devil.

9 No one who is born of God practices sin, because His seed abides in him; and he cannot sin, because he is born of God.

10 By this the children of God and the children of the devil are obvious: anyone who does not practice righteousness is not of God, nor the one who does not love his brother.

11 For this is the message which you have heard from the beginning, that we should love one another;

12 not as Cain, who was of the evil one and slew his brother. And for what reason did he slay him? Because his deeds were evil, and his brother's were righteous.

1 JOHN 2:1

My little children, I am writing these things to you so that you may not sin. And if anyone sins, we have an Advocate with the Father, Jesus Christ the righteous.

• Are you practicing sin? What is sin? Look at 1 John 3:4.

• According to verse 9, no one born of God spends time doing what? Why not? ("Born of God" is in the perfect tense.)

• According to verse 10, what two characteristics make children of the devil obvious? (By the way, the word *love* in verses 10 and 11 is also present tense in the Greek.)

• Now review what you have learned about the children of God and the children of the devil.

• Can a child of God sin? Look at 1 John 2:1. The verb *sin* is in the aorist tense and is therefore speaking of singular acts of sin. In 1 John 3:9, sin is in the present tense. What's the difference?

• Now when a person looks at his life, according to 1 John, how can he tell who his Father is?

OBSERVE

Let's continue to walk through 1 John 3. This time we'll examine verses 13-18.

Leader: Read 1 John 3:13-18 and have the group mark...

- *every reference to **knowing** and **abiding**.*
- *the words **love** ♡ and **hate** ♡⃠*

INSIGHT

The word translated as *love* in 1 John is the Greek word *agapao* (or one of its derivatives). This word carries the idea of an unconditional love, a love that has the highest good of the other person in mind. It's a love that isn't earned. This love is expressed even if the other person doesn't deserve it.

DISCUSS

- How do we know we've passed out of death into life, according to verse 14?

1 JOHN 3:13-18

13 Do not be surprised, brethren, if the world hates you.

14 We know that we have passed out of death into life, because we love the brethren. He who does not love abides in death.

15 Everyone who hates his brother is a murderer; and you know that no murderer has eternal life abiding in him.

16 We know love by this, that He laid down His life for us; and we ought to lay down our lives for the brethren.

17 But whoever has the world's goods, and sees his brother in need and closes his heart against him, how does the love of God abide in him?

18 Little children, let us not love with word or with tongue, but in deed and truth.

• How can you show that you love another person? Look at the places you have marked *love*. If love is so important to God, what are some practical ways we can show love to someone else?

• If you do not love, where do you abide (verse 14)?

• If you hate, do you have eternal life abiding in you (verse 15)? Why?

• Does John give us a middle ground between love and hate? Can you not hate but only avoid someone? Can you honestly say, "I love that person; I just won't have anything to do with her or him"? How does this relate to verse 18?

OBSERVE

Now let's look at the next several verses.

Leader: Read aloud 1 John 3:19-24.
  - *Mark **know**, **abide**, and **love** just as you've been doing.*

DISCUSS

- How does "we will know by this" in verse 19 relate to verses 17 and 18?

- What assurance does love like this bring to our hearts?

- What are two commands the Lord left us according to verse 23?

1 JOHN 3:19-24

19 We will know by this that we are of the truth, and will assure our heart before Him

20 in whatever our heart condemns us; for God is greater than our heart and knows all things.

21 Beloved, if our heart does not condemn us, we have confidence before God;

22 and whatever we ask we receive from Him, because we keep His commandments and do the things that are pleasing in His sight.

23 This is His commandment, that we believe in the name of His Son Jesus Christ, and love one another, just as He commanded us.

24 The one who keeps His commandments abides in Him, and He in him. We know by this that He abides in us, by the Spirit whom He has given us.

• What do you learn from marking *abides* in verse 24?

• According to all you have learned this week, what characterizes a true child of God?

WRAP IT UP

Are you a Christian? There is a lot of confusion about this question in the world. As you have seen from our study of God's Word, there is no confusion in Scripture. The characteristics of a believer are easy to observe, as are the characteristics of a nonbeliever.

What about you? Is God your Father? What about your family, your friends? The world screams, "Don't judge me!" Scripture already has. Love, obedience, abiding, and knowing God are the outward, obvious signs of a child of God. This is not confusing; the truth is plain and easy to observe.

Perhaps the Scriptures and the Holy Spirit have shown you that you are not a child of God. Why don't you give your life to Him right now? He loves you. He will meet you where you are and then He will change you. He will fill you with a love like you have never before experienced. Just pray to God, confess to Him the fact that you have sinned and are repenting, having a change of heart. That now you want to follow Him fully and, by the power of His Spirit, live righteously. If you give your life to Him, you will never be the same. You will never regret your surrender to Him, and you will know who your Father is. The world will know too, because you will begin to look like Him more and more in the way that you live, think, act, and talk.

Last week we saw first-hand what God's Word says about love and hate, about knowing God, and about knowing that He abides in us. It was an awesome study, but John still has more to say about loving, knowing, and abiding. This week you'll see for yourself how important love is to our heavenly Father. It's mentioned more than twenty times just in 1 John 4!

OBSERVE

Before we look at what God tells us about love, we need to know how to test the spirits to know if they are of God or not. Remember, we've seen that John wrote this letter because there were people, antichrists, who were seeking to deceive those who believed in Jesus.

Leader: *Read 1 John 4:1-6 aloud. As you read, have the group call out the following key words as they mark them:*
- *Mark references to **spirit**, including pronouns, with a cloud, like this:* 🞰
- *Mark **know** with a* **K.**

1 JOHN 4:1-6

1 Beloved, do not believe every spirit, but test the spirits to see whether they are from God, because many false prophets have gone out into the world.

2 By this you know the Spirit of God: every spirit that confesses that Jesus Christ has come in the flesh is from God;

3 and every spirit that does not confess Jesus is not from God; this is the spirit of the antichrist, of which you have heard that it is coming, and now it is already in the world.

4 You are from God, little children, and have overcome them; because greater is He who is in you than he who is in the world.

5 They are from the world; therefore they speak as from the world, and the world listens to them.

6 We are from God; he who knows God listens to us; he who is not from God does not listen to us. By this we know the spirit of truth and the spirit of error.

DISCUSS

• As you marked *spirit,* did it refer to one spirit? What contrasts did you see?

OBSERVE

Leader: *Have the group put a slash through every reference to the spirit that is not from God.*

DISCUSS

• What did you learn about the two different spirits?

• According to this passage, what is one of the ways you would recognize a false prophet?

• According to verse 4, who is greater?

• Look again at verse 4. Where does God live if I am His child?

• What did you learn by marking the word *know*?

OBSERVE

Leader: Read 1 John 4:7-11 aloud. As you read, have the group mark...

- *every occurrence of the word **love** with a heart.*
- *every reference to **God** with a triangle.*

DISCUSS

• How is God described in these verses?

• How is the love of God manifested (made recognizable, known) in verses 9-11?

• What else did you learn by marking *love*?

• How can knowing these truths about love help an individual?

• According to verses 7 and 8,
    whom are we to love?
    where does love come from?
    what is true of everyone who loves?
    what is true of one who does not love?

1 JOHN 4:7-11

7 Beloved, let us love one another, for love is from God; and everyone who loves is born of God and knows God.

8 The one who does not love does not know God, for God is love.

9 By this the love of God was manifested in us, that God has sent His only begotten Son into the world so that we might live through Him.

10 In this is love, not that we loved God, but that He loved us and sent His Son to be the propitiation for our sins.

11 Beloved, if God so loved us, we also ought to love one another.

1 JOHN 4:12-21

12 No one has seen God at any time; if we love one another, God abides in us, and His love is perfected in us.

13 By this we know that we abide in Him and He in us, because He has given us of His Spirit.

14 We have seen and testify that the Father has sent the Son to be the Savior of the world.

15 Whoever confesses that Jesus is the Son of God, God abides in him, and he in God.

16 We have come to know and have believed the love which God has for us. God is love, and the

OBSERVE

Leader: *Read aloud 1 John 4:13-21.*

- *Mark each reference to **abide** with a* .
- *Mark each reference to **know** with a* **K.**
- *Mark each reference to **love** with a* ♡.

DISCUSS

- What did you learn by marking *abide*?

- If I say that I love God, yet I hate my brother, what am I (verse 20)?

- If God so loved us, what should we do? Are you doing this?

- What did you learn by marking the word *know* in verses 13 and 16?

• What specifically did you learn about love?

• Why do we love?

OBSERVE

What can we learn about God from this passage?

Leader: Read 1 John 4:12-21 again.
  • *This time mark every reference to **God** with a triangle.*

DISCUSS

• What did you learn about God? Starting with verse 12, discuss what you learn about Him in each verse in this passage.

one who abides in love abides in God, and God abides in him.

17 By this, love is perfected with us, so that we may have confidence in the day of judgment; because as He is, so also are we in this world.

18 There is no fear in love; but perfect love casts out fear, because fear involves punishment, and the one who fears is not perfected in love.

19 We love, because He first loved us.

20 If someone says, "I love God," and hates his brother, he is a liar; for the one who does not love his brother whom he has seen, cannot love God whom he has not seen.

21 And this commandment we have from Him, that the one who loves God should love his brother also.

• What are the characteristics of a child of God, according to this passage? As before, start in verse 12 and discuss each verse individually.

OBSERVE

God is love. If we are children of God, we are to love both our brother and our enemy. But how much does God love us? Let's look at two other passages and try to answer this question.

JOHN 3:16

For God so loved the world, that He gave His only begotten Son, that whoever believes in Him shall not perish, but have eternal life.

Leader: Read aloud John 3:16 and Romans 5:6-8. Have the group mark...
  • *each reference to* **God** *with a triangle.*
  • *each reference to* **Christ** *with a cross.*

DISCUSS

• What did God do to prove His love for the world?

- When did Christ die for us?

- What did we do to earn Christ's death for us?

- What did you learn by marking *God*?

- What did you learn by marking *Christ*?

- How much does God love you?

- Does this surprise you? Is it different from what you thought? How does it make you feel?

- How would this knowledge affect your willingness to love others? How would this love manifest itself?

ROMANS 5:6-8

6 For while we were still helpless, at the right time Christ died for the ungodly.

7 For one will hardly die for a righteous man; though perhaps for the good man someone would dare even to die.

8 But God demonstrates His own love toward us, in that while we were yet sinners, Christ died for us.

WRAP IT UP

Are you beginning to get a glimpse of how much God loves you and how much He intends for you to show love to the world around you? Love is best expressed by action—and how well God expressed it! He gave the supreme gift: His only begotten Son. God loves you so much that, while you were still His enemy, Christ died for you.

Now then, if Christ is in us and we are in Christ, is it too much for us to love our brother? our neighbor? our enemy? We can tell whose child we are by the way we love.

Oh friend, abide in Him, walk in the light, walk in love.

In this our last week together, we will examine the fifth and final chapter of 1 John. We will look one more time at ways you can know that you know that God is your Father.

OBSERVE

Let's start with the first five verses.

Leader: Read 1 John 5:1-5 aloud. As you read, have the group mark...
- *every reference to **love** with a ♡.*
- *every reference to **know** with a **K.***
- *every occurrence of the word **overcome** with a half circle and an arrow, like this:* ⌒↘
- *the phrases **born of God** and **born of Him**. Use a half-circle, like this:* ⌣

DISCUSS

- According to verse 1, what are two characteristics of a child of God, one born of Him?

1 JOHN 5:1-5

1 Whoever believes that Jesus is the Christ is born of God, and whoever loves the Father loves the child born of Him.

2 By this we know that we love the children of God, when we love God and observe His commandments.

3 For this is the love of God, that we keep His commandments; and His commandments are not burdensome.

⁴ For whatever is born of God overcomes the world; and this is the victory that has overcome the world—our faith.

⁵ Who is the one who overcomes the world, but he who believes that Jesus is the Son of God?

• What do you learn about overcoming from verses 4 and 5? How do you think this would be lived out practically?

• In case you missed it, who is it that overcomes the world?

• Have you overcome the world? Or does the world overcome you? If the latter is true, what's your status with God? Are you His child or not?

• According to these five verses, what is true about every person who is born of God, who has God as his or her Father?

OBSERVE

Let's look at the next several verses together. Although these verses are theologically complicated and can be explored much more deeply, we want to see what they tell us in respect to knowing who our Father is.

Leader: *Read 1 John 5:6-12.*
- *Mark each reference to* ***Jesus Christ*** *with a cross.*
- *Mark references to* ***testify*** *and* ***testimony*** *with a rectangle:* ☐

DISCUSS

- What do you learn from marking references to *testify* and *testimony*?

- To what do the Holy Spirit and God testify or bear witness?

1 JOHN 5:6-12

6 This is the One who came by water and blood, Jesus Christ; not with the water only, but with the water and with the blood. It is the Spirit who testifies, because the Spirit is the truth.

7 For there are three that testify:

8 the Spirit and the water and the blood; and the three are in agreement.

9 If we receive the testimony of men, the testimony of God is greater; for the testimony of God is this, that He has testified concerning His Son.

10 The one who believes in the Son of God has the testimony in himself; the one who does not believe God has made Him a liar, because he has not believed in the testimony that God has given concerning His Son.

11 And the testimony is this, that God has given us eternal life, and this life is in His Son.

12 He who has the Son has the life; he who does not have the Son of God does not have the life.

• According to verse 10, the one who believes in the Son of God has what within himself?

• The Spirit bears witness, according to verse 7. Therefore who is within the believer?

• What characteristic of a child of God is revealed in this passage?

• What did you learn about Jesus Christ?

• What do you learn about yourself from this passage?

OBSERVE

Leader: *Read 1 John 5:13-21 and have the group mark...*

- *each occurrence of the word **know**.*
- *each reference to **sin(s)**.*
- *every reference to **eternal life** by underlining it.*

DISCUSS

- What did you learn by marking the word *know*?

- What did you learn from marking *eternal life*? How does this parallel 1 John 5:11-12?

- How can you know that you have eternal life?

- What are some of the characteristics of a child of God that we've seen in these past six weeks?

- What did you learn by marking the word *sin*?

1 JOHN 5:13-21

13 These things I have written to you who believe in the name of the Son of God, so that you may know that you have eternal life.

14 This is the confidence which we have before Him, that, if we ask anything according to His will, He hears us.

15 And if we know that He hears us in whatever we ask, we know that we have the requests which we have asked from Him.

16 If anyone sees his brother committing a sin not leading to death, he shall ask and God will for him give life to those who commit sin not leading to death. There is a sin leading to death; I do not say that he should make request for this.

17 All unrighteousness is sin, and there is a sin not leading to death.

18 We know that no one who is born of God sins; but He who was born of God keeps him, and the evil one does not touch him.

19 We know that we are of God, and that the whole world lies in the power of the evil one.

• What do verses 14-15 teach you about prayer?

• Based on what you have studied in 1 John, why would God answer prayer?

INSIGHT

The meaning of verses 16 and 17, which refer to committing "a sin leading to death," is debated among scholars. It does seem clear, however, that if I find a brother in sin, I should pray for him. Since we don't know what the "sin leading to death" is, we should pray every time we find a brother in sin.

• According to verse 18, what are the characteristics of a child of God?

• If I belong to God, who keeps me from sin (giving me the power not to sin, not to live in habitual sin)?

• Now look back again at verse 13. Why did John write these things?

• Do you know, beloved, if you have eternal life? If not, then tell God that you want it, that you want to turn from the world—from your sin—to Him and be set free. Ask Him to make you righteous and He will. And remember, the victory that overcomes with world will be your faith.

20 And we know that the Son of God has come, and has given us understanding so that we may know Him who is true; and we are in Him who is true, in His Son Jesus Christ. This is the true God and eternal life.

21 Little children, guard yourselves from idols.

WRAP IT UP

What are the characteristics of a child of God? You have already seen them, but let me ask you:

- Are you walking in obedience to the Father?
- Are you walking in obedience to the Word?
- Is the Holy Spirit present in your life?
- Are you loving your brother? your neighbor? your enemy?

If you are, then you can know, based on 1 John, that God is your Father. If these things are not true in your life, then who is your father?

Why don't you take time to pray as a group, even silently. Maybe someone present wants to have God as his or her Father, to be born into His family, to receive forgiveness of sins and eternal life. If so, simply tell God you repent, you are changing your mind and are going to believe in Jesus Christ, receiving Him as your Savior and your God, your Lord. God said, as many as receive Jesus Christ, to them He gives the power to become a child of God (John 1:12).

Now, may God bless you and give you a hunger to study His Word. May God give you a hunger for the bread of life and the discipline to study even when you don't feel hungry.

This unique Bible study series from Kay Arthur and the teaching team of Precept Ministries International tackles the issues with which inquiring minds wrestle—in short, easy-to-grasp lessons ideal for small-group settings. These first five study courses in the series can be followed in any order. Here is one possible sequence:

How Do You Know God's Your Father?
by Kay Arthur, David and BJ Lawson
This six-week study looks at the change that takes place when a mortal human encounters a holy God. It focuses on John—who went from being a "son of thunder" to being "the disciple Jesus loved." The student will walk through the book of 1 John, taking note of the characteristics of a child of God versus those of a child of the devil.

Having a Real Relationship with God
by Kay Arthur
For those who yearn to know God and relate to Him in meaningful ways, Kay Arthur opens the Bible to show the way to salvation. With a straightforward examination of vital Bible passages, this enlightening study focuses on where we stand with God, how our sin keeps us from knowing Him, and how Christ bridged the chasm between humans and their Lord.

Being a Disciple: Counting the Real Cost
by Kay Arthur, Tom and Jane Hart
Jesus calls His followers to be disciples. And discipleship comes with a cost, a commitment. This study takes an inductive look at how the

Bible describes a disciple, sets forth the marks of a follower of Christ, and invites students to accept the challenge and then enjoy the blessings of discipleship.

How Do You Walk the Walk You Talk?

by Kay Arthur

This thorough, inductive study of Ephesians 4 and 5 is designed to help students see for themselves what God says about the lifestyle of a true believer in Jesus Christ. The study will equip them to live in a manner worthy of their calling, with the ultimate goal of developing a daily walk with God marked by maturity, Christlikeness, and peace.

Living a Life of True Worship

by Kay Arthur, Bob and Diane Vereen

Worship is one of Christianity's most misunderstood topics. This study explores what the Bible says about worship—what it is, when it happens, where it takes place. Is it based on your emotions? Is it something that only happens on Sunday in church? Does it impact how you serve? This study offers fresh, biblical answers.

ABOUT KAY ARTHUR AND PRECEPT MINISTRIES INTERNATIONAL

Kay Arthur, executive vice president and cofounder of Precept Ministries International, is known around the world as a Bible teacher, author, conference speaker, and host of national radio and television programs.

Kay and her husband, Jack, founded Precept Ministries in 1970 in Chattanooga, Tennessee. Started as a fledgling ministry for teens, Precept today is a worldwide outreach that establishes children, teens, and adults in God's Word, so that they can discover the Bible's truths for themselves. Precept inductive Bible studies are taught in all 50 states. The studies have been translated into 65 languages, reaching 118 countries.

Kay is the author of more than 120 books and inductive Bible study courses, with a total of over 5 million books in print. She is sought after by groups throughout the world as an inspiring Bible teacher and conference speaker. Kay is also well known globally through her daily and weekly television and radio programs.

Contact Precept Ministries International for more information about inductive Bible studies in your area.

Precept Ministries International
P.O. Box 182218
Chattanooga, TN 37422-7218
800-763-8280
www.precept.org

ABOUT DAVID AND BJ LAWSON

David and BJ Lawson serve as directors of the Teen/College Ministry of Precept Ministries International. Both have been involved in Precept Ministries since the early 1980s and became staff members in 1997. David, a former police officer and pastor in Atlanta, is a coauthor with Kay Arthur and others of the *International Inductive Study Series* and a teacher on the *Precept Upon Precept* videos. BJ is a speaker and teacher for conferences and seminars.